The Covenant of
YAHUSHA
In the Book of the
SEVENS

Kel "The WordSmith" Rhyne

Cover Design: Kel Rhyne

Publishing by 2 the Kingdom LLC

ISBN: 979-8-9880101-0-4

Printed in the United States of America

Table Of Contents

SECTION 1

Wisdom and Armor of Yah

Hebrew Names and Word Meanings

Elohim: GOD

El *(short)***:** God

El Elyon: GOD is Most High

El Shaddai: GOD is Almighty

Yahuah: GOD's name - I AM "Eternal"

Yah *(short)***:** God's name - I AM "Eternal"

Yahuah Elohim: I AM "Eternal" God

Adonai: LORD (greater)

Baal: Lord (lesser)

Adonai Elohim: the LORD God

Yahusha: Yah is Salvation

Yeshua *(short)***:** Savior - *{Joshua}*

Ha'Mashiach: The Anointed One

Ruach: Spirit

Ruach Ha'Qodesh: The Holy Spirit

YahQodesh: Yah is Holy

Qoddishkem: Holy / Set Apart / Sanctified Ones

Yashar'el: Israel / Straight Line or Path to God

Yahudah: Judah / Thanksgiving

YAHUAH and the "Spark" of Creation

What does Yahuah mean:
Yahuah means "to Exist", as in, I AM, I WAS, and I WILL BE. In a single word, "Eternal".

Before the Beginning of Creation... YAHUAH IS. Completely Full, All Encompassing, and Absolute in Existence. There is only the Eternal State of Yahuah, without Beginning and without End! Yahuah Alone is Eternal and besides Him, there is No Other... ***"I AM Yahuah, and there is no other; There is no Elohim (God) besides Me."*** <u>*Isaiah 45:5*</u>

The Beginning of Creation:
Yahuah, while in the mist of His Eternity, *Chooses* to exercise His Absolute Power by way of Sharing Himself and Expanding His Nature. His Absolute Will, in an Absolute way, Chooses to generate the Essence of Holy and Absolute LOVE. This "Love" of Yahuah is the "Spark" of Spiritual and Physical Creation. Yahuah's Desire of Love is/was so strong and deep that it moved the Spirit of His Might to *push out* from His Eternal State and ***"Elohim Created the Heavens*** (Space & Time) ***and the Earth*** (Solid & Liquid Matter). ***"And the earth was without form and void and darkness was on the face of the deep and the Spirit of Elohim moved upon the face of the waters."*** Now, Yahuah's Wisdom of Love is/was so quick and precise that it moved the Spirit of His Word to speak; ***"And Elohim said, Let there be light"***; and light burst forth from the Heavens and from the Earth. And the Space, Time, Earth, and Water radiated magnificently with a pure spiritual light. ***"And Elohim saw that the light was good: and Elohim separated the light from the darkness. And Elohim called the light Day, and the darkness He called Night. and the evening and the morning were the first day."*** <u>*Genesis 1:1-5*</u>

- Understanding The Choice -
The Knowledge of Good & Evil

Then Yahuah Elohim took the man and put him in the Garden of Eden to tend and keep it. And he Yahuah Elohim commanded the man, saying, "Of every tree in the garden you may freely eat; but of the tree of the knowledge of good and evil you shall not eat, for in the day that you eat of it, you shall surely die". (Genesis 2:15-17)

After the creation of women, according to the book of Jubilees, *Yahuah Elohim* wanted to see what His greatest creations (Humans) would do concerning the tree of the knowledge of good & evil. So *Yahuah Elohim* called forth the angel "*Mastema*" (Satan) to report to Him what the man & woman would do regarding the Tree in the midst of the Garden. *Yahuah Elohim* did not instruct the angel on how he should do this but allowed Mastema to have freedom of choice concerning the matter. Just as *Yahuah* had made the man in the image of Himself, so too did He make the animals in the image of the angels, with the serpent bearing a likeness to the angel Mastema. Now, the serpent being the most subtle (clever) beast of the field chose to use "subtle" deceit. The serpent approached the woman and questioned her knowledge about "the Tree" and then presented a Deceitful but Tempting option, saying to her, "You shall not surely die, for *Elohim* knows that in the day you eat it your Eyes will become Opened, and you will be like Him, Knowing Good and Evil". So when the woman saw that the tree was good for food, that it was pleasant to the sight, and a tree desirable to make one wise, she took of its fruit and ate. She also gave it to her husband and he ate it. Then the Eyes of both of them were opened, and they knew that they were Naked..." (*Genesis 3:1-7*). Then, Mastema promptly went to *Yahuah Elohim* and stated what the man & woman had done.

After Adam had eaten the fruit, both his and Eve's *Physical Eyes* were opened. They could see each other's physical bodies and thus their nakedness. They had gained the ability of physical awareness... they could tell the difference between *Yahuah Elohim* and themselves; the difference between Eternal & Mortal; between Spirit & Body; and between Faith & Fear. They could now comprehend the finite span of mortal life and would eventually experience a mortal death.

Then Yahuah Elohim said, "Behold, the Man has become like one of Us, to know Good and Evil. And now, lest he put out his hand and take also of the Tree of Life, and live forever" - therefore Yahuah Elohim drove out Man and placed a Cherubim at the east of the Garden and a Flaming Sword which turned every way, to guard the Way of the Tree of Life. (Genesis 3:22-24)

Adam and Eve being made in the Image of Yah already had *Thought*, *Desire*, and *WILL*, which allowed them the Freedom of Choice. After eating from the Tree of the Knowledge of Good and Evil, they gained the ability to know the differences between *Spiritual & Physical* existence and to select between things that will bring them *Health & Life* or *Sickness & Death*. Every person born into this world has inherited this ability and it is up to each person to decide what they will have... that which is Good or that which is Evil. Every person *WILL* receive just what they have freely chosen, whether for Better or for Worse. So, the "*Choice of Life*" is between these two options; Choosing the *Spirit of Yah*, that is Holy (Pure & Continuous) Love; which creates, nurtures, and maintains Life... or Choosing *Self over Yah*, that is Vice (Selfish Indulgence); which takes away, dissolves, and brings to desolation, the object of desire.

The Choice is Yours! So Choose Life! That You and Your Descendants May Live! Deuteronomy 30:19

YAHUAH and the Name Change

The Name of Yahuah:
In the beginning, the Creator refers to Himself as *Elohim* or *El* for short. During the time of Moses, He reveals His name as *Yahuah* or *Yah* for short. After Israel's rebellion, the kingdom of Yah split into two nations. Northern Israel (10 Tribes) was defeated by the Assyrians and enslaved among the nations of the world. Roughly 250 years later, the southern nation of Judah (2 Tribes) was conquered and carried away by the Babylonians. During this time they were forced to learn a new language and many Judaens were defiling themselves with Babylonian practices. The priests of Judah did not want Yahuah's name to be defiled among the Babylonians because they regarded Yah's name as highly sacred. So as they were translating their scriptures, they decided to change Yah's name from "Yahuah" to "Adonai" which means "the LORD".

The Name of Yahusha:
After the siege and destruction of Jerusalem, the people were scattered and their possessions were taken. The Judaen Sadducee captives along with Roman scholars translated the old and new testaments into Greek. When it came to the name *Yahusha*, instead of simply transferring it over into Greek, they used a method called transliteration, which is the conversion of words from one alphabet to another using the swapping of letters. They used the shortened version of his name "*Yeshua*" and transliterated that into Greek as "*Iesous*". Then later it was transliterated into Latin as "*Iesus*"... and then one more time in the late 1500s into English as "*Jesus*".

Yeshua translated to English is Joshua.

The Savior's name is NOT Jesus! It is *Yahusha* or *Yeshua* for short.

The Significance Of Number 7

Number seven is one of the most significant and symbolic numbers in the Bible. It has been used in numerous contexts throughout Scripture and has held a great deal of meaning for millennia. From the Seven Days of Creation to the Seven Bowls of Wrath, the number seven is an integral part of the Bible and has been used to convey a great deal of information.

The number seven is denoted as the number of completeness and perfection. This can be seen in the seven days of creation, where Yah creates the world and declares it to be very good. In the book of Revelation, seven is mentioned numerous times, indicating that it is a key number in the spiritual realm. Seven is also stated in the Ten Commandments, where Yahuah says, to remember the Sabbath (Seventh-day) and keep it holy.

In the Old Testament, seven is used as a sign of divine perfection. It is shown through the seven Holy Days with the Feast of Unleavened Bread, Feast of Trumpets, and Feast of Tabernacles, each lasting for seven days.

The number seven is also used to denote the power of Yah. The Lamb appearing before the throne as though it had been slain, had seven horns. Horns in scripture are a metaphor for power. The seven stars in the right hand of Yahusha in the book of Revelation signify His power over the 7 churches.

The number seven is also used to represent the seven deadly sins. These sins are pride, envy, gluttony, greed, sloth, wrath, and lust. In scripture, these sins are the very roots of evil and must be avoided to maintain a life of virtue, joy, peace, and love.

7 Armors Of YAH

Put on the Whole Armor Of YAH

Ephesians 6:10-18 & Isaiah 59:17

The Shield of Faith

The Helmet of Salvation

The Cloak of Zeal

The Sword of the Spirit

The Belt of Truth

The Breastplate of Righteousness

Feet Prepared with the Gospel of Peace

Picture/Glenn Arekion Ministries

11

Armor of YAH

Shoes of Peace:

The Shoes of Peace are for Spiritual Mobility. They symbolize the peace of Yah which passes all understanding. It is a reminder of the ultimate peace that comes from aligning our lives with Yah's will and trusting in His plans for us. The Shoes of Peace represent the readiness of a soldier to go wherever Elohim leads them and to be ready for whatever Yahusha calls them to do.

Belt of Truth:

The Belt of Truth is for Spiritual Steadfastness. It is a reminder to live in honesty, integrity, and to stand firm in the truth of Yah's Word. The belt of truth binds the rest of the armor together, showing that our faith and trust in Yahusha are the foundation of everything else. The Belt of Truth is a symbol of our commitment to living honestly and standing firm in our faith.

Breastplate of Righteousness:

The Breastplate of Righteousness is for Spiritual Strength. It readies us to live a life of righteousness and consistency, as Yah has called us to do. The Breastplate of Righteousness protects our spiritual vital points from the strikes of the enemy, reminding us that Yah will defend us and that we can trust in His righteousness and goodness.

Helmet of Salvation:

The Helmet of Salvation is for Spiritual Fortitude. As we engage the spiritual battle, it aids us in being vigilant, staying alert, and keeping our minds focused on Yahusha for salvation. The Helmet of Salvation is also a reminder of the hope that we have in Yahusha Ha'Mashiach for protection and guidance.

Cloak of Zeal:

The Cloak of Zeal is for Spiritual Zest. It symbolizes the passion and enthusiasm with which we are to operate in the ways of Yahusha. It is a reminder to be passionate about our faith and to be zealous in our exercising of His Covenant.

Shield of Faith:

The Shield of Faith is for Spiritual Defense. It is a reminder to stay strong in our faith and to trust in the Lord's protection. It is for taking refuge in Yahusha, as faith in Him is a strong shield against the wiles of the enemy. And it is a reminder to stay focused and to trust His plans for our lives.

Sword of the Spirit:

The Sword of the Spirit is for Spiritual Offense. With it, we speak against the enemy's attacks and stand firm on Yah's Word. It reminds us to be spiritually prepared and to fight the enemy's lies and deceptions with Truth. The Sword of the Spirit is both powerful & effective, and when used correctly, has the power to subdue all opponents. We are to stay strong in our faith and use the Word to fight the good fight.

Section 2

Bible Timeline, Covenants, & Holy Days

Bible Timeline Summary

Books of the Bible - Enoch - Jubilees - Jasher

4000 BC

- The Creation of Heavens & Earth - 1st 5 days of Creation (Space, Time, Earth, Water, and Light,)

- The Formation of Heavens, Seas, Dry Earth, Plants, Sun, Moon, Birds, and Fish

- The Creation of Man & Sabbath Rest - 6th & 7th day (Land Animals, Man, and Rest)

- The Fall of Man

- The First Death

- The Trespass of 200 Angels (Azazel & Semjaza + 200)

- The Nephilim

- The Judgement of the Fallen Angel (through Enoch)

2300 BC - Noah & the Flood

1st Covenant - *Noahide*

2250 BC - Demonic Spirits bound & Mastema (Satan) given 10% of demons to use.

-   Book of Healing and Demonic Reversals - Written by Angels - Given to Noah - Passed on to Shem (who becomes Melchizedek)

2200 BC - Nimrod - New Nephilim - Tower of Babel

15

2000 BC - Abraham & Idols

2nd Covenant - _Abrahamic_

1900 BC - Melchizedek (King/Priest of God Most High) Blesses Abraham

- Sodom & Gomorrah

- Issac

- Esau & Jacob

1750 BC - Joseph Sold into Egyptian Captivity

1500 BC - Moses to Pharaoh

- Passover to Mt. Sinai

3rd Covenant - _Mosaic / Sinai_

- 40 Years in the Desert - Promised Land

- Battle of Jericho

- Judges: Gideon, Samson, Ruth to Samuel

- Kings: Saul & David

- David's Sin

4th Covenant - _Davidic_

1000 BC - Solomon's Reign - Builds Temple of Yah

- Yah's People Split - Two Kingdoms - Israel (10 Tribes) & Judah (2 Tribes)

950 to 725 BC - Israel (16 kings) - Judah (16 kings) - 18 total Prophets

722 BC - Israel Conquered & Enslaved by the Assyrians (Nephilim nation) - **Lost 10 Tribes** - Scattered among nations

586 BC - Judah Captured by Babylonians - Nebuchanazzer

536 BC - Babylonians conquered by Persia - Darius the Great - *Zoroastrian (Mazda) leader*

538 BC - Judah Lead back to Jerusalem by Darius

450 BC - City Rebuilt

250 BC - The Old Testament translated into Greek

0 BC - Word of Yah placed into the Virgin Mary / Birth of Immanuel / Yahusha - Son of Yah

   - 3 Magi / Wisemen - (Melchior, Gasper, & Balthasar) - Priests of the Order of Melchizedek (modern-day Mazdaism) - Followed the North Star to pay homage and anoint the newborn King and High Priest, Yahusha Ha'Mashiach

   - Early Life of Yahusha

30 AD - The Baptism, Mission, Teaching, and Work of Yahusha

5th Covenant - *Yahushanic*

33AD - The Sacrifice and Resurrection of Yahusha

55 AD - Epistles of Paul

60 AD - Letters of Peter, James, and John

70 AD - Siege of Jerusalem

95 AD - John Exiled

312 - Constantine's Vision

321 - The Day of Worship changed from the Sabbath to Sunday

487 - Rome Declines as a Nation

610 - Start of Islam - A New Religion

632 - Muhammad dies.

656 - The Quran is written.

800 - Charlemagne - Start of the Holy Roman Empire

950 - Conversion of the Khazar Kingdom

1095 - 1291: The Roman Crusades

1147 - The Waldensian Movement

1517 - The Protestant Reformation

1539 - The Bible Assembled

1540 - The Society of Jesus or Jesuits is Started

1480 - 1580 - Transatlantic Slave Trade

Late 1500s America - 90% of Native Aboriginals Die of Diseases

1607 - The Pilgrims Arrive at Jamestown, VA

1613 - America's 1st Plantation: *Shirley Plantation*

1619 - African Captives Arrive at Virginia

1620 - The Puritans Arrive at Boston, MA

1620 - Sunday (Blue) Laws Established in America

1622 - First Africans (considered indentured) arrive at Shirley Plantation

1645 - The Rosicrucian Writings

1692 - Salem Witch Hunt Trials

Whole 17th century - The Transatlantic Slave Trade in Full Swing

1712 - "*The Making Of A Slave*" - Unethical / Psychological / Torturous Human Conditioning introduced by Willie Lynch

1717 - England's Masonic Grand Lodge

1752 - Benjamin Franklin's Kite and Key Experiment

1775 - The American Revolutionary War

1776 - United States declares independence from England

1806 - The Fall of the Holy Roman Empire

1808 - The Transatlantic Slave Trade is Banned in America.

1849 - Harriet Tubman and the Underground Railroad

1861 - 1865: American Civil War - The Emancipation Proclamation

1866 - 14th Amendment passed, but is not upheld until 1965

1865 - 1877: - Racial Violence after the Civil War

1870 - 1914: - The American Industrial / Technological Revolution

1871 - District of Columbia (UNITED STATES) Corporation Act

1883 - Unjust Civil Rights Cases

1883 - 1955: White Supremacy - The KKK - And Destruction

1914 - 1918: - World War 1

1917 - Central Banking Act *(America)*

1929 - The Lateran Treaty made with Rome

1929 - 1939: The Great Depression

1932 - The Tuskegee Syphilis Experiment on Black Males

1935 - Social Security Act and Welfare Programs Begins

1939 - 1945: World War 2

1948 - White Ashkenazi Jews become the Nation of Israel - False Israel

1955 - Civil Right Movement starts - Rosa Parks Bus Boycott

1955 to 1975: Vietnam War

1963 - March on Washington for Jobs and Freedom - "I Have a Dream" Speech, MLK

1964 - Civil Rights Act passed

1965 - Voting Rights Act passed

1968 - Martin Luther King, Jr. Assassinated

1970s - 1980s: - Cocaine / Crack Epidemic begins

1971 - War on Drugs Starts

1970s to 2010s - Mass Incarceration of Black Males

1985 - Black Liberation Organization Bombed

1986 - First Private Prison at State Level Opens

1988 to 2009 - The Rise and Perpetuation of Gangsta Rap

2001 - World Trade / Planes Crashes / War on Terror Starts

2001 - 2021 - War in Afghanistan

2003 - 2011 - War in Iraq

2014 - 2021: War in Iraq 2 - War Ended - much military equipment left behind

2020 to 2022 - COVID Pandemic, but still ongoing

2023 - Ongoing - World Leaders push for ***"The Great Reset" - A System of World Wide Control***
 - A One World Government Under Techno - Ecclesiastical Tyranny
 - Artificial Intelligence - NeruLink - Robotics - RFID - Block chain - Crypto - Virtual / Augmented Reality
    Intrusive Surveillance - Pod Housing - Bug Diet - Owning Nothing)

-----Revelation & the Prophets-----

Possibly the Season - Near Present? - 7 Seals - Rise of
the 1st & 2nd Beast Systems -

   - 144,000 sealed - Great Tribulation - 7 Trumpet Blasts

   - Return of the Yahusha / 1st Resurrection / 144,000 Rise
and Change

   - 7 Bowls of Wrath Poured Out on the Evil Kingdom -
(Wrath of Yah)

   - Casting of the Anti-Christ and False Prophet into the Lake
of Fire - Satan Bound for 1000 years

   - Judgement of the Living

6th Covenant - Millennial?

   - Yah's Kingdom Established - 1000 Years of Peace - King
Yahusha and the Saints Rule

   - After 1000 Years Satan is Loosed

   - Deception and Destruction of Gog & Magog (nations of
the world) through Holy Fire from YAH

   - 2nd Resurrection (from Adam to last of Magog)

   - Judgement of the Dead - Man, Nephelium, and Fallen
Angels

   - 2nd Death (Lake of Fire) for Satan, Fallen Angels,
Nephilim, Wicked Men, and Death

- Creation of New Heaven, Earth, and Jerusalem

7th Covenant - Everlasting?

- The Spread of Yahuah's Everlasting Kingdom Without End

7 Great Covenants

The 7 Covenants Reveal Yah's Grand Design To Save Mankind From Sin and Establish His Eternal Kingdom on Earth.

Source Book(s): Genesis 9

Great Covenant Number: 1

Covenant Name: Noahide Covenant

Passed Down From: Yahuah Elohim - Yahuah Elyon

Given To: Noah And All Living Creatures

Mediated By: None

Terms of Agreement: Be Fruitful And Multiply

Covenant Law:
Not To Eat Flesh With Blood In It, & Blood For Blood Law

Covenant Promises:
Will Not Destroy The Earth With Water Again - Rainbow As A Sign & Fulfilled Promise

Covenant Status: Active / Fulfilled

The Need: To Start Over And Make Peace Between Elohim And The Earth

The Purpose: To Start The Plan Of Salvation

24

7 Great Covenants

Source Book(s): Genesis 15, 17

Great Covenant Number: 2

Covenant Name: Abrahamic Covenant

Passed Down From:
Yahuah Elohim - Yahuah Elyon - Yahuah Shaddai

Given To: Abraham - Issac - Jacob *(Israel)*

Mediated By: None

Terms Of Agreement: Belief - Credited As Righteousness

Covenant Law: Circumcision *(Cutting of the Foreskin)*

Covenant Promise:
Will Raise Up A Nation From His Offspring

Covenant Status: Active / Fulfilled

The Need: Someone To Believe In Elohim

The Purpose: To Make A People / Nation / Kingdom

7 Great Covenants

Source Books: The Pentateuch - Genesis, Exodus, Leviticus, Numbers, Deuteronomy

Great Covenant Number: 3

Covenant Name: Torah - The Law - 1st
(Hebrews 8-9,)

Passed Down From: Yahuah Elohim - Yahuah Elyon
(Exodus 31:18, Deuteronomy 9:10, Luke 11:20)

Given To: The People of Israel at Mt. Sinai
(Deuteronomy 9:10)

Mediated By: Moses
(Exodus 3:18, Deuteronomy 9:10)

Terms of Agreement: Obedience
(Deuteronomy 5:1, Deuteronomy 12:32)

Covenant Law: 10 Commandments + (603) Commands, Judgements, Statues, & Ordinances
(Deuteronomy 20 - Book of Leviticus)

Covenant Promises: Protection & Guidance
(Deuteronomy 28:6)

Covenant Status: Active / Fulfilled

The Need: To place His Law on Earth.

The Purpose: To make His people a Nation and so that mankind would be without excuse from sin.

7 Great Covenants

Source Books(s): 2 Samuel 7

Great Covenant Number: 4

Covenant Name: Davidic Covenant

Passed Down From: Yahuah Elohim - Yahuah Elyon

Given To: David

Mediated By: None

Terms of Agreement: To Love the Law

Covenant Law: To Continue In Obedience of the Law

Covenant Promise:
Will Bring Forth the Savior *(Yahusha)* through his Bloodline

Covenant Status: Active / Fulfilled

The Need: Someone to Love the Law

The Purpose: To bring forth the Savior (Yahusha) into the Earth.

7 Great Covenants

Source Books: New Testament Pentateuch (Matthew, Mark, Luke, John, & Acts)

Great Covenant Number: 5

Covenant Name: *Yahusha's Covenant* - New Covenant - 2nd
(Matthew 26:28, Mark 14:24, Luke 22:20, 2 Corinthians 3:6)

Passed Down From: Yahuah Elohim - Yahuah Shaddai - Father
(Hebrews 8:8, John 6:32, John 17:23)

Given To: All of Mankind
(1 John 2:2, John 3:16, Galatians 3:28)

Mediated By: Yahusha - Yeshua - Word of Yah - Son of Elohim
(Hebrews 12:24)

Terms of Agreement: **Faith - Repentance - Baptism**
One Must Believe in Yahusha as Savior!
(Romans 3:22, Galatians 2:16, Galatians 3:22)

Covenant Law: 4 Parts - Command, Judgement, Appointment, and Duty

(1) Perfect Command - To **Love** Your Neighbor As Yeshua Has Loved You.

(1) Judgement - To **Repent** *(making use of Prayer, Fasting, and Scripture Study)*

(1) Appointed - To **Develop 12 Fruits** of the Holy Spirit

(1) Duty - To **Do Good Works**

(John 13:34, John 15:16, Ephesians 2:10, Ephesians 5:1)

Covenant Promises: **7 Fold Holy Spirit**, **Kingdom Of Yah**, and **Salvation**

28

The Need: To Save Mankind From Sin.

The Purpose: To Call And Set Apart The Governing Class (First Saints) Of The Kingdom.

Yahusha's Covenant
Terms of Agreement - Extended

1. Proclamation of Faith

One is to **Believe and Proclaim** that Yahuah is who HE says HE is... The ONE and ONLY Elohim. Creator and sustainer of the Heavens and Earth. And that Yahusha Ha'Mashiach, is who He says He is... The Only Begotten Son and Word of Yahuah Elohim... the Anointed vessel sent to Save Mankind from its Sin.

2. Confession & Repentance of Sin

One is to agree that they have Trespassed (Sinned) against Yahuah... **Confess** and **Ask for Forgiveness** of those sins and **desire a change** from selfish ways. Then one is to accept Yahusha's Sacrifice (Death on the Cross) for Forgiveness of Sin.

3. Full Emersion Baptism

As the **Outward sign** of the **Inward change,** one is to undergo a Baptism. The full submersion baptism is symbolic of putting to death (*through a watery burial*) the old self with its way of life, and resurfacing as a "new" person, starting a new way of life in the way of Yahusha. *"Truly, truly, I say to you, unless one is born again he cannot see the kingdom of Yah." John 3:3*

29

Yahusha's Covenant
Covenant Law - Extended

(1) Perfect Command: *To Love One Another As Yahusha Has Loved You.*

A new commandment I give to you, that you *love one another*, as *I have loved you*, that you also *love one another*.
John 13:34

My command is this: *Love each other* as *I have loved you*. *John 15:12*

These things I command you, that you *love one another*.
John 15:17

---

(1) Judgement: *To Repent*

Yahusha began to preach saying, *"Repent,* for the kingdom of heaven is at hand." *Matthew 4:17*

I have not come to call the righteous, but sinners to *repentance*." *Luke 5:32*

Therefore *repent* and return, so that your sins may be wiped away, in order that times of refreshing may come from the presence of the Lord. *Acts 3:19*

"Repent and be baptized, every one of you, in the name of Yahusha Ha'Mashiach for the forgiveness of your sins. And you will receive the gift of the Holy Spirit. *Acts 2:38*

---

(1) Appointed: *Develop The 12 Fruits Of Holy Spirit*

You did not choose Me, but I chose you and appointed you that you should **go and bear fruit**, and that your fruit should remain, that whatever you ask the Father in My name He may give you. *John 15:16*

"I am the vine, you are the branches. He who abides in Me, and I in him, **bears much fruit**; for without Me you can do nothing. *John 15:5*

By this My Father is glorified, that you **bear much fruit**; so you will be My disciples. *John 15:8*

---

(1) Duty: *To Do Good Works*

For we are His workmanship, created in Yahusha Ha'Mashiach for **good works**, which God prepared beforehand that we should walk in them. *Ephesians 2:10*

"Who is wise and understanding among you? Let him show by **good conduct** that **his works** are done in the meekness of wisdom." *James 3:13.*

"That those who have believed in Yah should be careful to maintain **good works**." *Titus 3:8.*

Yahusha's Covenant
Covenant Promises - Extended

1. 7 Fold Holy Spirit:

And I will pray the Father, and He will give you another Helper, that He may abide with you forever - the Spirit of Truth, whom the world cannot receive, because it neither sees Him nor knows Him; but you know Him, for He dwells with you and will be in you. **John 14:16-17**

The 7 Fold Holy Spirit is the Spirit Structure of Yah. He is the guide, free gift, and down payment of the Kingdom; The Holy Spirit grants access to a portion of Kingdom Life features, such as: An "Energized" Attitude, Consistent Behavioral Patterns, Heightened Linguistics, Talents, Abilities, and at the Purest levels... "Spiritual Power" (Asking In Yahusha's Name with the request Actually Happening!)

For more information on development of Soul and Spirit... Please See Pages: **62 - 74**

1. Kingdom of Yah:

Fear not, little flock, for it is your Father's good pleasure to give you **the kingdom**. *Luke 12:32*

"But seek first **His kingdom** and **His righteousness**, and all these things will be given to you as well." - *Matthew 6:33*

"For the **kingdom of Yah** is not a matter of eating and drinking, but of righteousness, peace and joy in the Holy Spirit." - *Romans 14:17*

Pray then like this: "Our Father in heaven, hallowed be your name. **Your kingdom come**, your will be done, on earth as it is in heaven." *Matthew 6:9-10*

The Kingdom of Yah is: The Spiritual Reality of Yahuah! A reality where the Essence of Love in all its Glory reigns supreme. The Kingdom <u>IS</u> His Spiritual Structure and His Righteousness <u>IS</u> His Love. "Man" is made in the image and likeness of Yahuah, and as such, is fashioned with a similar Soul Structure, one made from Spirit & Earth. Through the Teachings of Yahusha and Guidance of the Holy Spirit, a person is encouraged to develop "LOVE", which is a portion of the kingdom of Yah.

3. **Salvation:**

And this is the will of Him who sent Me, that everyone who sees the Son and believes in Him may have everlasting life; and I will **raise him up** at the last day. *John 6:40*

And there is **salvation** in no one else; for there is no other name under heaven that has been given among men by which we must be saved." Acts 4:12

For by grace you have been **saved through faith**, and that not of yourselves; it is the gift of God, not of works, lest anyone should boast. *Ephesians 2:8-9*

Man has utterly sinned against Yahuah, is found totally guilty of breaking His Torah law, and is deemed worthy of Condemnation and Death! Yahusha offers Salvation through repentance and baptism for the forgiveness of Sin. This "forgiveness", which is a free gift, saves the believer's soul from damnation, which is the Lake of Fire also called the 2nd Death. Salvation happens for each individual during Final Judgement after the 2nd Resurrection.

7 Great Covenants

Source Scripture(s): Ezekiel 37:24-28

Great Covenant Number: 6

Covenant Name: Millennial Covenant ?

Passed Down From: Yah the Son - The Most High King & Priest - Lord Yahushua

Given To: Those Living During The Millennium

Mediated By: The Saints - Royal (King) Priests, Greater Priests, & Lesser Priests

---

Terms of Agreement: ?

Covenant Law: ?

Covenant Promises: 1000 Years of Peace & Prosperity on the Earth

Covenant Status: Not Yet Given

The Need: ? To set up the government for the first 1000 years of the Kingdom.

The Purpose: ? To train the citizens of the Kingdom in the ways of Yah?... Not Yet fully known.

7 Great Covenants

Source Scripture(s): Revelation 21

Great Covenant Number: 7

Covenant Name: Everlasting Covenant ?

Passed Down From: Yahuah Elyon - Yahuah Shaddai

Given To:
Those Living After The Great Throne Judgement -
Those Who's Names Are Written In The Lamb's Book Of
Life

Mediated By: N/A

Terms of Agreement: ?

Covenant Law: ?

Covenant Promises:
New Heaven, Earth, and City of Jerusalem - Everlasting
Life

Covenant Status: Not Yet Given

The Need: ? Not Yet Known.

The Purpose: To Establish the Holy Everlasting Kingdom
- for Eternity

7 Holy Days

The Holy Days picture Yah's Plan to save Israel and represents the season in which it takes place.

1. **The Passover** - *Status: Fulfilled*

Passover is an important festival that is celebrated by Hebrew people around the world as a commemoration of the freeing of the Israelites from slavery in Egypt. The festival takes place on the 15th day of the Hebrew month of Nisan. This usually falls between March and April in the Gregorian calendar.

Passover is celebrated by Hebrew people to remember the biblical story of the "Exodus" which states that Yah freed the Israelites from slavery in Egypt after they had been oppressed by the Pharaoh for over 400 years. According to the Bible, Yah sent 10 plagues to Egypt to convince the Pharaoh to let the Israelites go and the final plague was the death of the firstborn of each family. The Israelites were instructed to mark their doorposts with the blood of a sacrificed lamb so that the angel of death would pass over their homes and spare them. Thus, the name Passover.

The festival of Passover typically begins with a special dinner, called a seder, which includes a variety of symbolic foods. These foods are meant to remind the participants of the different aspects of the Exodus story. A seder plate will usually include bitter herbs, which symbolize the bitterness of slavery in Egypt, a roasted egg to signify sacrifice, and a lamb shank bone to symbolize the sacrifice of the paschal lamb.

During the seder dinner, participants will recite prayers, read passages from the Torah, and drink four cups of wine to represent the four promises Yah made to the Israelites during the Exodus.

At the end of the seder, participants will sing traditional songs. The holiday of Passover lasts for seven days, as it is linked to the Feast of Unleavened Bread, and is typically observed with special meals and activities that commemorate the Exodus story.
(Leviticus 23:5)

New Covenant Meaning: Pictures Yahusha as the Sacrificial Lamb shedding His blood for the sins of mankind.

2. **The Feast of Unleavened Bread** - *Status: Fulfilled*

The Feast of Unleavened Bread is a Hebrew festival that takes place during the 7 days of Passover. It is one of the three pilgrimage festivals that Hebrews were commanded to celebrate in the Torah, along with the Festival of Weeks and the Festival of Booths. The Feast of Unleavened Bread is observed by eating only unleavened bread, or matzah, during the seven days of the festival. This symbolizes the haste in which the Israelites had to leave Egypt, without being able to wait for their bread to rise.

The Feast of Unleavened Bread begins on the 15th day of the Jewish month of Nisan, which is usually in April or May. This day is known as the first day of Passover, or Pesach. During the seven days of the festival, Jews abstain from eating any leavened bread products. This includes bread, cake, crackers, and other baked goods. They are also forbidden from owning or possessing any leavened bread during this time. This is to remind them of the haste in which their ancestors had to leave Egypt.

The last day of the festival is the 21st of Nisan, which is known as the seventh day of Passover. This day is known as the "Great Sabbath" and is marked by a special prayer service.

The Feast of Unleavened Bread is a reminder of the miraculous deliverance of the Israelites from bondage in Egypt. It is a time to remember their faith and trust in Elohim and to look forward to a new season of joy, hope, and redemption. *(Leviticus 23:6-14)*

New Covenant Meaning: Pictures a Disciple's duty to remove sin from their daily lives.

3. **The Pentecost** - *Status: Fulfilled*

Originally known as the Feast of Weeks or day of First Fruits, this is a celebration to Yahuah for the bounty of the spring harvest. The men of Israel were to take the first fruits of their harvest (called bikkurim), travel to Jerusalem, and offer it as a sacrifice at the temple.

Pentecost means fiftieth, as it is the number of days between Passover and this holy day. It is the anniversary of Yahuah giving the Torah to Israel at Mt. Sinai and is the holy day that marks the descent of the Holy Spirit upon the Apostles and other followers of Yahusha. It is celebrated fifty days after Passover, on the seventh Sunday after Resurrection Sunday and ten days after Ascension Day. Pentecost is also known as the "Birthday of the Church", as it marks the day that the Church was born.

In the book of Acts, the Apostles were gathered together in one place, then the Holy Spirit descended upon them, "suddenly there came from Heaven a sound like the rush of a mighty wind and it filled all the house where they were sitting. And there appeared to them tongues as of fire, distributed and resting on each one of them. And they were all filled with the Holy Spirit and began to speak in other tongues, as the Spirit gave them utterance."

Pentecost is seen as a day of great joy and celebration, as it marks the gift of the Holy Spirit given to believers. It is a time for followers of Yahusha to celebrate the presence of the Holy Spirit and to remember the work of Yahusha Ha'Mashiach. It is also a time for believers to rededicate themselves to the faith and duty of their covenant and to remember the mission of Yahusha. Pentecost is a time of renewal and hope, and a time to recommit ourselves to the Way of Love. (*Leviticus 23:15-22*)

New Covenant Meaning: Pictures the Disciples of Yahusha receiving Yahuah's Holy Spirit.

4. **The Feast of Trumpets** - *Status: Next Event To Come!*

The Feast of Trumpets, also known as Rosh Hashanah, is a Hebrew holy day celebrated annually on the first day of the Hebrew month of Tishrei. The holiday marks the beginning of the Hebrew New Year, and it is traditionally observed with special prayers, rituals, and observances.

The festival is traditionally celebrated with a series of prayers, special liturgies, and the blowing of the shofar (ram's horn). The celebration is also marked with the dipping of apples in honey, which is meant to symbolize a sweet new year.

The Feast of Trumpets is considered a solemn occasion, as it is a time to reflect on the coming year and to repent of any wrongs that may have been committed during the past year. It is also a time to rejoice in the hope of a better future.

The history of the festival dates back to the time of Moses, when the Israelites were commanded to observe the first day of the seventh month of the Hebrew calendar as a day of rest and to sound the shofar as a reminder of the covenant between Yah and the people of Israel. This holy day also foretells of a series of events in the future called the 7 Trumpets Blasts.

Today, the Feast of Trumpets is a time for celebration, reflection, and renewal. Families come together to enjoy special meals, recite prayers and blessings, and remember their heritage and the promises of Yah. It is a time for all Hebrews to come together and celebrate the joys and challenges of life. (Leviticus 23:23-25).

New Covenant Meaning: Pictures a time of war, plagues, and tribulation concluding with Yahusha's Return.

5. **The Day of Atonement** - *Status: Event Coming!*

The Day of Atonement, also known as Yom Kippur, is an important Hebrew holy day observed annually on the 10th day of the Hebrew month of Tishrei. It is the holiest and most solemn day of the year for the Hebrew people and is marked by 25 hours of fasting, prayer, and repentance. The Day of Atonement is a day of self-reflection and repentance, and it is believed that Yah will forgive all sins committed during the previous year on this day if the people fully repent and seek forgiveness.

The Day of Atonement is the 5th holy day mentioned in the Torah and is observed by Jews (Hebrews) around the world. The day begins with a special prayer service in which the people ask Yah to forgive them for their sins. As part of the repentance process, Jews also abstain from eating and drinking for 25 hours, as well as refraining from work. During this time, Jews also give charity and recite special prayers.

At the end of the day, a special priestly service is performed in the Temple in Jerusalem. During this ritual, the priest enters the innermost chamber of the Temple and sprinkles blood from a sacrificed bull and goat on the altar to symbolize the people's repentance. This ritual is known as the "Kapparot" and is believed to be the moment when Yah pardons the sins of the people in the old covenant.

The Day of Atonement is a powerful reminder of the importance of self-reflection and remembrance of sin in the Torah, as well as the power of Yah's forgiveness and mercy. It is a day for Jews to reflect on their actions of the past year and to make a commitment to live a better life in the coming year. *(Leviticus 23:26-32)*

New Covenant Meaning: Pictures the binding of Satan at the beginning of the Millennium, the Judgement of Sin, and beginning of the Kingdom of Yahusha.

6. **The Feast of Tabernacles** - *Status: Coming After That!*

A seven-day celebration of the great fall harvest, observed by dwelling in temporary booths for the duration of the Feast. The Feast of Tabernacles, also known as Sukkot, is an important holy day that is celebrated in the fall of the year. It is a time of joy and celebration and is one of the three pilgrimage festivals that Hebrews are commanded to observe. The Feast of Tabernacles is a commemoration of the years that the Israelites spent in the wilderness, and is a reminder of the shelter and protection that Yah provided them during that time. It also represents the future 1000 years of "Peace on Earth" under the Kingship of Yahusha, where the knowledge of Yah will fill the earth even as the waters fill the seas.

During the end of the festival, it was a tradition that the congregation circles the synagogue seven times while holding branches of willow, myrtle, and palm, and prayers and readings are recited. When the final portion of the

Torah is read, the festival is concluded and the cycle is ready to begin again. This is a time of great celebration, with singing and dancing.

The Feast of Tabernacles is a time of joy & celebration, a time to remember the protection & provision of Yah and to look forward & be ready for the coming kingdom. (Leviticus 23:33-43)

New Covenant Meaning: Pictures the 1000-year Millennium, when the earth will be ruled by Yahusha and His Saints.

7. **The Last Great Day** - *Status: Coming After 1000 Year Kingdom!*

The Last Great Day is the eighth and final day of the Feast of Tabernacles, which is a seven-day observance that takes place on the 15th day of the seventh month in the Jewish calendar. It is a day of joy and hope, as it represents the end of the Fall Festival and the beginning of a new spiritual year. The Last Great Day is also known as the Great Day of the Lord, and it is a day of great celebration.

The Last Great Day is a day of rejoicing because it marks the end of the world and the beginning of a New Era of Eternity. The day is symbolic of the final judgment that will take place when Yahusha brings justice to everyone. On this day, all of creation will be judged, and everyone will receive the rewards for their deeds. The Last Great Day is also a day of hope because those who have accepted Yahusha will be saved and enter the Kingdom, while those who have not will be eternally separated from Yah.

The Last Great Day is special because it is a time for reflection and spiritual growth. On this day, Believers in Yahusha are encouraged to focus on their relationship with Yah and to reflect on their lives. They are also encouraged to share their faith with others, to pray for their family, friends, and neighbors, and to give thanks for all the blessings in their lives.

The Last Great Day is a reminder of Yah's love and mercy, and it is a reminder of the eternal life that awaits those who accept Yahusha as their Lord and Savior. (Leviticus 23:36-39).

New Covenant Meaning: Pictures the coming "2nd Resurrection and Great Throne Judgment", at which time, all of humanity will be raised from the dead (Adam to the last of Magog) and will be Judged according to thier works.

SECTION 3

7 Churches, Seals, Trumpets, And Bowls

7 Letters to the 7 Churches
Revelations Chapter 2

1st Letter to: **Ephesus** - *The Loveless Church*

These are the words of Him who holds the Seven Stars in His Right Hand, who walks in the mist of the Seven Golden Lampstands:

"I know your works, your labor, your patience, and that you cannot bear those who are evil. And you have tested those who say they are apostles and are not, and have found them liars; and you have persevered and have patience, and have labored for My name's sake and have not become weary. Nevertheless I have this against you, that you have left your first love. Remember therefore from where you have fallen; repent and do the first works, or else I will come to you quickly and remove your lampstand from its place—unless you repent. But this you have, that you hate the deeds of the Nicolaitans, which I also hate.

He who is has an ear, let him hear what the Spirit says to the Churches. **To him who Overcomes, I will grant to eat from the Tree of Life, which is in the midst of the Paradise of Elohim.**

2nd Letter to: **Smyrna** - *The Persecuted Church*

These are the words of the First and the Last, who Died and came to Life again:

"I know your works, tribulation, and poverty (but you are rich); and I know the blasphemy of those who say they are Jews and are not, but are a synagogue of Satan. Do not fear any of those things which you are about to suffer. Indeed, the devil is about to throw some of you into prison, that you may be tested, and you will have tribulation ten days. Be faithful until death, and I will give you the crown of life.

He who is has an ear, let him hear what the Spirit says to the Churches. **He who Overcomes, Shall Not be hurt by the Second Death.**

<u>3rd Letter to:</u> **Pergamos** - *The Compromising Church*

These are the words of Him who wields the Sharp Two-Edged Sword:

"I know your works, and where you dwell, where Satan's throne is. And you hold fast to My name, and did not deny My faith even in the days in which Antipas was My faithful martyr, who was killed among you, where Satan dwells. But I have a few things against you, because you have there those who hold the doctrine of Balaam, who taught Balak to put a stumbling block before the children of Israel, to eat things sacrificed to idols, and to commit sexual immorality. Thus you also have those who hold the doctrine of the Nicolaitans, which thing I hate. Repent, or else I will come to you quickly and will fight against them with the sword of My mouth.

He who has an ear, let him hear what the Spirit says to the Churches. **To him who Overcomes, I will give to eat of the Manna that is Hidden, and I will give him a White Stone with a New Name engraved on the stone, which no one knows or understands except he who receives it.**

<u>4th Letter to:</u> **Thyatira** - *The Corrupt Church*

These are the words of the Son of Elohim, who Eyes that Flash like a Flame of Fire, and whose Feet Shine like Fine Brass:

"I know your works, love, service, faith, and your patience; and as for your works, the last are more than the first. Nevertheless I have a few things against you, because you allow that woman Jezebel, who calls herself a prophetess, to teach and seduce My servants to commit sexual immorality and eat things sacrificed to idols. And I gave her time to repent of her sexual immorality, and she did not repent. Indeed I will cast her into a sickbed, and those who commit adultery with her into great tribulation, unless they repent of their deeds. I will kill her children with death, and all the churches shall know that I am He who searches the minds and hearts. And I will give to each one of you according to your works.

To him who Overcomes and keeps My Works until the end, to him I will give Authority and Power over the Nations; and he shall rule them with a Scepter of Iron, they shall be dashed to pieces like the potter's vessels, as I also have received from My Father; and I will give him the Morning Star.

He who has an ear, let him listen and heed what the Spirit say to the Churches.

5th Letter to: **Sardis** - *The Dead Church*

These are the words of Him who has the Seven Spirits of Elohim and the Seven Stars:

"I know your works, that you have a name that you are alive, but you are dead. Be watchful, and strengthen the things which remain, that are ready to die, for I have not found your works perfect before Yah. Remember therefore how you have received and heard; hold fast and repent. Therefore if you will not watch, I will come upon you as a thief, and you will not know what hour I will come upon you. You have a few names even in Sardis who have not defiled their garments; and they shall walk with Me in white, for they are worthy.

To him who Overcomes shall be clothed in White Garments, and I will Not Erase or Blot Out his name from the Book of Life; I will acknowledge him and I will confess his name openly before My Father and before His Angels.

"He who has an ear, let him hear what the Spirit says to the churches."

6th Letter to: **Philadelphia** - *The Faithful Church*

These are the words of the Holy One, the True One, He who has the Key of David, who Opens and no one Shuts, who Shuts and no one Opens:

"I know your works. See, I have set before you an open door,

and no one can shut it; for you have a little strength, have kept My word, and have not denied My name. Indeed I will make those of the synagogue of Satan, who say they are Jews and are not, but lie—indeed I will make them come and worship before your feet, and to know that I have loved you. Because you have kept My command to persevere, I also will keep you from the hour of trial which shall come upon the whole world, to test those who dwell on the earth. Behold, I am coming quickly! Hold fast what you have, that no one may take your crown.

To him who Overcomes, I will make him a Pillar in the Sanctuary of My Elohim; he shall Never be put out of it or go out of it, and I will write on him the name of My Elohim, the name of the city of My Elohim, the New Jerusalem, which descends from My Elohim out of Heaven, and I will write on him My New Name.

"He who has an ear, let him hear what the Spirit says to the churches."

7th Letter to: **Laodicea** - *The Lukewarm Church*

These are the words of the Amen, the Faithful and True Witness, the Origin and Beginning of the Creation of Elohim:

"I know your works, that you are neither cold nor hot. I could wish you were cold or hot. So then, because you are lukewarm, and neither cold nor hot, I will vomit you out of My mouth. Because you say, 'I am rich, have become wealthy, and have need of nothing'—and do not know that you are wretched, miserable, poor, blind, and naked— I counsel you to buy from Me gold refined in the fire, that you may be rich; and white garments, that you may be clothed, that the shame of your nakedness may not be revealed; and anoint your eyes with eye salve, that you may see. As many as I love, I rebuke and chasten. Therefore be zealous and repent. Behold, I stand at the door and knock. If anyone hears My voice and opens the door, I will come in to him and dine with him, and he with Me.
.

To him who Overcomes, I will grant him to sit beside Me on My Throne, as I Myself Overcame and sat down beside My Father on His Throne.

"He who has an ear, let him hear what the Spirit says to the churches." 48

7 Seals
Revelation Chapter 6

1st Seal: *The Rider on the White Horse:*

The first seal from the book of Revelation is found in Revelation 6:1-2. It is a powerful and symbolic image that conveys Elohim's power and authority over the world.

The seal is described as a white horse, its rider having a bow and a crown. The ride has the power to conquer. This imagery is often interpreted as symbolizing the anti-christ's rise to power, victory over nations, and authority over the world without the bloody violence of traditional warfare. The rider has a form of rulership, as he is given a crown.

2nd Seal: *The Rider on the Red Horse:*

The second seal from the book of Revelation is a vision of a red horse, with its rider carrying a great sword. This horseman has been given the power to take peace from the earth and to bring about a great conflict. The rider is seen to have a mission to bring about war and death, with the sword representing the bloodshed and destruction that will come with it.

This passage is a warning of the great wars that are to come in the last days. The rider is a symbol of the great forces at work trying to bring about chaos and destruction, while peace is taken away. The sword is a sign of the violence and death that will be part of the war. The red horse is a warning that the world will be filled with conflict and bloodshed.

3rd Seal: *The Rider on the Black Horse:*

The third seal of Revelation shows a vision of a black horse ridden by a figure with a pair of scales in his hand. The rider's voice cries out "A quart of wheat for a denarius, and three quarts of barley for a denarius, and do not harm the oil and the wine!" This imagery is a warning of the future lack, of food shortages, and rations.

The rider is a symbol of judgment, balancing the scales of justice. The price of wheat and barley given by the rider shows that the cost of food will be extremely high. This means that the famine will be severe and people will have to pay exorbitant prices to feed their families. The rider's warning not to harm the oil and wine is also a sign of judgment. Oil and wine were considered luxuries and it was a warning against wasting resources that could be used to help others in need.

4th Seal: *The Rider on the Pale Horse:*

The fourth seal found in the book of Revelation is one of the most chilling and powerful seals of the seven. It is a sign of the coming of death and destruction to the world.

As the fourth seal is opened, a pale green horse emerges from the darkness. Sitting atop the horse is a figure known as Death, who is accompanied by Hades. Together they are given power over a fourth of the Earth to kill by sword, famine, disease, and wild beasts of the earth.

5th Seal: *The Cry of the Martyrs*

The fifth seal of the book of Revelation is found in chapter 6, verses 9-11. It is a powerful vision of the souls of martyrs who were slain for their faith in Yah. The fifth seal is a reminder of the ultimate sacrifice that many have made for their faith and its ongoing cost.

The passage begins with a vision of a great multitude of

martyrs standing before the throne of Elohim. These souls are described as being dressed in white robes, a symbol of their innocence and purity.

They cry out to Elohim for justice and vindication, asking "How long, O Lord, holy and true, dost thou not judge and avenge our blood on them that dwell on the earth?" They are told to be patient, for their time of vindication is coming. The voice then gives the martyrs white robes and tells them to rest a little longer, until the full number of their fellow servants and their brethren who were to be killed as they had been, should also be completed.

6th Seal: *Cosmic Disturbances - 144,000 Sealed*

The sixth seal from the book of Revelation is described in Revelation 6:12-14. This seal marks a time of great cosmic upheaval and disturbance. The heavens are opened and a great earthquake occurs, the sun turns black, the moon turns to blood, and the stars of the sky fall to the earth.

The opening of the sixth seal is a time of great fear and trembling. It is a time of judgment and destruction. It is a time when Yah's wrath is unleashed on the earth, and the entire creation trembles at his anger.

The sun turns black like sackcloth, a sign of Yah's judgment and anger. The moon turns to blood, a sign of Yah's wrath and judgment. Stars of the sky fall to the earth, a sign of Yah's power and authority.

The effects of the sixth seal are far-reaching. All of creation is affected by this cosmic disturbance and the earth itself is shaken. All the people on earth will be filled with terror, and the kings of the earth, the great ones, the rich, and the mighty will hide in the caves and amongst the rocks of the mountains. All the nations of the earth will be filled with fear and dread. After which an Angel ascending for the rising of the Sun, having the Seal of the Living Elohim... Seals 12 thousand from each of the 12 Tribes of Israel in their foreheads.

7th Seal: *Prelude to the 7 Trumpets*

The seventh seal of the book of Revelation is one of the most mysterious and profound seals mentioned in the Bible. It is the last and final seal before the seven trumpets are unleashed.

The seventh seal is described in the book of Revelation 8:1-2, which reads: "And when he had opened the seventh seal, there was silence in heaven about the space of half an hour. And I saw the seven angels which stood before Yah; and to them were given seven trumpets."

The seventh seal is a time of silence and reflection in heaven before the seven angels blow their trumpets and begin their mighty blasts.

The opening of the seventh seal also marks the beginning of a period of judgment for the world. The seven angels, who were given the seven trumpets, will blow their trumpets to announce the coming of Yah's wrath and judgment for all those who have not accepted Him.

7 Trumpets
Revelation Chapter 8

1st Trumpet Blast: *The Vegetation is Struck:*

The first Trumpet Blast of Revelation is a powerful and loud sound that shakes the earth. It is a sound so loud that it sets off a chain reaction of events that cause great destruction and chaos.

The first Trumpet Blast is described in Revelation 8:7, which reads "The first angel sounded, and there followed hail and fire mingled with blood, and they were cast upon the earth: and the third part of trees was burnt up, and all green grass was burnt up." This passage indicates that the first Trumpet Blast causes a combination of hail, fire, and blood to be cast upon the earth. The hail, fire, and blood cause a third of the trees and all of the green grass to be burned up.

2nd Trumpet Blast: *The Seas are Struck:*

The second Trumpet Blast from the book of Revelation is a great and terrible sound that brings about a great and terrible event. It is as if a great mountain had been thrown into the sea, and its impact is felt similarly.

Something like a large mountain burning with fire falls into the sea, causing a third of the sea to become blood. This event brings death to a third of all living creatures in the sea.

3rd Trumpet Blast: *The Waters are Struck:*

The third Trumpet Blast from the book of Revelation is one of the most devastating of the seven trumpet blasts. This blast is described in Revelation 8:10-11:

"The third angel blew his trumpet, and a great star fell from heaven, blazing like a torch, and it fell on a third of the rivers and on the springs of water. The name of the star is Wormwood. A third of the waters became wormwood, and many people died from the water because it had been made bitter."

This trumpet blast is incredibly destructive, as it causes a great star to fall from heaven and turn a third of the waters of the earth into bitter, poisonous wormwood. This would have a catastrophic effect on the environment, as the rivers and springs of water become unsafe to drink. Those who rely on these waters for sustenance would be left thirsty and malnourished as a result of the pollution.

The name of the star that falls, Wormwood, is symbolic of bitterness and sorrow. The mention of this name foreshadows the coming destruction and suffering that will be caused by the third Trumpet Blast.

The effects of this blast would be widespread, as the rivers and springs of water are essential components of the earth's ecosystems. The destruction of these resources would be devastating to the environment and to the creatures that depend on them for life. It would also take a heavy toll on the human population, as the water would be rendered undrinkable and many people would die as a result.

4th Trumpet Blast: *The Heaven is Struck:*

The Fourth Trumpet Blast from the Book of Revelation is described as the luminary bodies being struck.

"The fourth angel blew his trumpet, and a third part of the sun was smitten, and a third part of the moon, and a third part of the stars; so as a third of them was darkened, and the day did not shine for a third part of it, and the night likewise."

This trumpet blast strikes the sun, moon, and stars decreasing the amount of the light given off from them by 1/3.

Immediately following this is an angel with a loud voice flying in the midst of heaven saying: Woe, Woe, Woe to the inhabitants because of the next 3 trumpets blasts, for they are great and powerful.

5th Trumpet Blast: *1st Woe - The Locust from the Bottomless Pit*

 The fifth trumpet blast from the book of Revelation is a terrifying and destructive event. It is the first of the three "Woe" judgments, which is described in Revelation chapter 9:1-12.

When the fifth trumpet blows, an angel falls from heaven to earth and lands at the door of the Abyss. The angel has the key to the Bottomless Pit and opens it. Out of the Abyss comes a great cloud of smoke, which darkens the sky and blocks out the sun and the air. Out of the smoke come locusts, described as having the appearance of horses prepared for battle. The locusts are commanded not to harm any grass, plants, or trees, but only those people who do not have the seal of Elohim on their foreheads.

The locusts have a leader, who is called the Abaddon, the Destroyer. The locusts have crowns of gold on their heads, faces like men, hair like women, and teeth like lions. They wear breastplates of iron have wings and their tails sting like scorpions. They are given power to hurt people for five months.

The locusts cause a great amount of pain and torment to those who do not have the seal of Elohim on their foreheads. The pain is so great that people will seek death, but not find it. The torment lasts for five months, and anyone who does not have the seal of Yah on their forehead cannot find relief from the pain.

6th Trumpet Blast: *2nd Woe - The Angels from the Euphrates River*

The 6th Trumpet Blast from the book of Revelation is the 2nd of the woes.

The 6th angel sounds his trumpet and releases the four angels bound at the River Euphrates. These angels are destroyers and are unleashed with the power to slay a third of mankind. Their horses release fire, smoke, and sulfur that come from their mouths, and they use these elements to bring forth death and destruction.

But even after this event, those who were not killed still refused to repent of their many sins.

During the time of the trumpet blast, power is given to Yahusha's "**Two Witnesses**". They have a ministry that lasts 42 months. They have the power to open shut the sky for rain and can strike the earth with plagues similar to those in Egypt as often as they choose. They are clothed in sackcloth and will take on the "Beast from the Bottomless Pit". They will be overcome by the beast, but after 3 days the breath of life shall quicken them and they shall rise to meet Yahusha in the air.

7th Trumpet Blast: *3rd Woe - Yah's Kingdom Proclaimed!* *- Prelude to the 7 Bowls of Wrath*

The seventh trumpet blast from the book of Revelation is

the 3rd Woe and is one of the most momentous blasts of the seven.

This blast is the last of the seven and signifies the return of Yahusha.

The seventh trumpet blast is described as a loud and powerful sound coming from heaven, like the sound of many waters, thunder, and lightning. This sound is so powerful that every living creature, both in heaven and on earth, hears it. It is a call to all of creation to recognize the ultimate victory of Elohim over evil and to prepare for the coming judgment.

The seventh trumpet blast opens the temple in Heaven where a great and wondrous sign of a woman ready to give birth to a male child; is clothed with the sun & moon with 12 stars under her feet and in the presence of a great red dragon that stands ready to devour the child as soon as it is born... this trumpet blast also releases the 7 angels having Yah's final earthly judgments: the 7 Bowls of Wrath.

Revelation Chapter 10 - 16

Note - The Lamb (Yahusha) and the 144,000 standing on Mount Zion... they sing a new song that only they can learn.

7 Bowls of Wrath
Revelation Chapter 16

1st Bowl Poured Out: *Loathsome Sores:*

The first Bowl of Wrath from the book of Revelation is a vivid and powerful image of divine judgment. It is described in Revelation 16:2, "And the first went and poured out his bowl upon the earth; and it became a noisome and grievous sore upon the men which had the mark of the beast, and upon them which worshiped his image."

This bowl symbolizes a severe and painful punishment that is inflicted upon those who have chosen to submit to the Beast. This punishment is described as a "noisome and grievous sore", which is likely a type of painful skin infection or ulcer. This punishment is extremely painful and debilitating, leaving those affected in agony and despair. The severity of this punishment is indicative of Yah's displeasure and serves as a warning to those who choose to reject Him.

Furthermore, this punishment is specifically targeted at those who have "the mark of the beast" and who "worshipped his image". This indicates that this punishment is directed at those who have willingly embraced the Beast's power and authority. This punishment serves as a reminder that Yah will not tolerate those who choose to reject Him and His teachings.

2nd Bowl Poured Out: *The Seas Turn to Blood:*

The second Bowl of Wrath from the book of Revelation is one of the most devastating and destructive judgments, as described in the Bible. This bowl of wrath is poured out upon all the seas, turning them into blood. As it says in Revelation 16:3, "The second angel poured out his bowl into the sea, and it became like the blood of a dead man, and every living creature in the sea died."

This terrible judgment is a sign of Yah's wrath and anger. It is an intense punishment for the evil and wickedness of the people who have disobeyed Yah and his commands. The sea, which is usually full of life and beauty, has been turned into a dead and lifeless wasteland. Every single living creature, from the smallest fish to the largest whale, has perished in this judgment.

3rd Bowl Poured Out: *The Waters Turn to Blood:*

The third Bowl of Wrath, as described in the book of Revelation, is an apocalyptic event of great magnitude. It is described as the third angel pouring out his vial on the rivers and fountain of fresh water, turning them into blood. This means that all the water sources of the earth are no longer drinkable, and all of the creatures dwelling in them will die.

The imagery of this event is one of great destruction, with rivers and springs of water turning to blood and all living creatures in them dying. This is a reminder of the plagues that Yah sent upon Egypt in the Old Testament, and of the power of Yah to bring destruction upon those who defy Him. The effect of this Bowl of Wrath is indeed great and wise for the angel says, "Because they (the unrepentant) have shed the blood of the "saints and prophets", therefore, you have given them blood to drink, for they are worthy of such treatment.

4th Bowl Poured Out: *Men are Scorched:*

The fourth bowl of wrath is fearsome and destructive, it is poured out upon the earth. In this bowl, a great and powerful angel is commanded to pour out his vial onto the sun, causing it to scorch the earth with intense heat and radiation. This intense heat causes the earth to be parched and dried up, and the people to be scorched and burned. All vegetation and trees are dried up and burned, and the rivers and seas become like blood, full of dead and dying creatures that were unable to survive in the harsh environment.

The effects of the fourth bowl of wrath are devastating. The intense heat and radiation cause the people to suffer horribly, and the environment is so hostile that they utterly blaspheme Elohim, who has power over the plagues; so they did not repent of their inequities or give Yah glory.

5th Bowl Poured Out: *Darkness and Pain*

The fifth Bowl of Wrath from the book of Revelation is a powerful and terrifying punishment from Yah. It brings judgment upon those who are willfully sinful and unrepentant.

The fifth angel pours out his vial on the seat of the beast. His entire kingdom is plunged into thick darkness. But lo, this is no ordinary darkness. This darkness has a power of pain within it, so intense that the inhabitants of the evil kingdom will gnaw their tongues in agony. Despite this pain, they continue to blaspheme, will not turn from their wicked ways, and will not repent!

6th Bowl Poured Out: *Euphrates River Dried Up*

The sixth bowl of wrath from the book of Revelation is the last vial of judgment and destruction. The sixth bowl of wrath is poured out onto the great river Euphrates and its water is dried up. This symbolizes the removal of obstacles and hindrances to the march of the evil forces of the Beast, who are coming to wage war against the saints.

The sixth bowl of wrath also brings forth three evil spirits, like frogs, from the mouths of the dragon, the beast, and the false prophet. These frogs represent demonic forces, which have been released to deceive the people of the earth with their lies and deceptions. This is in order to gather them together for the final battle, which will be fought against the Lamb in the Valley of Armageddon.

The sixth bowl of wrath also brings forth a great earthquake that shakes the entire earth. This earthquake is a sign of the coming judgment of Yah against all those who have rejected His truth and His way of life.

Note Yahusha says, *"Behold, I am coming as a thief. Blessed is he who watches..."*

7th Bowl Poured Out: *The Earth Utterly Shaken*

The seventh bowl of wrath, as outlined in the book of Revelation chapter 16:17-21, is the last of the seven bowls that were poured out by seven angels upon the earth. It is the most severe of all the bowls of wrath, and its effects are devastating.

Immediately upon the pouring of the seventh bowl, the world is shaken by a great earthquake that is so powerful that it splits the mountains and islands, and the cities of the world are laid waste. The fountains of the great deep are broken up, and the windows of heaven are opened, allowing the rains to pour down from the sky in a torrential deluge.

At the same time, this bowl unleashes a great voice from the throne of Yah, saying "It is done." This voice is followed by lightning, thunder, and voices, and a great earthquake so strong that it divides the city into three parts. This is followed by an equally great hailstorm that pounds the earth with hail as big as a talent and this hail is powerful and exceedingly great! But still the wicked continue to blaspheme Elohim and will not repent of their many sins.

SECTION 4
-MENORAH Charts-
Illustrations Of The
7 FOLD HOLY SPIRIT
And Additional Writings

7 Fold Holy Spirit, 7 Churches, 7 Covenants, 7 Holy Days, 7 Days of Creation

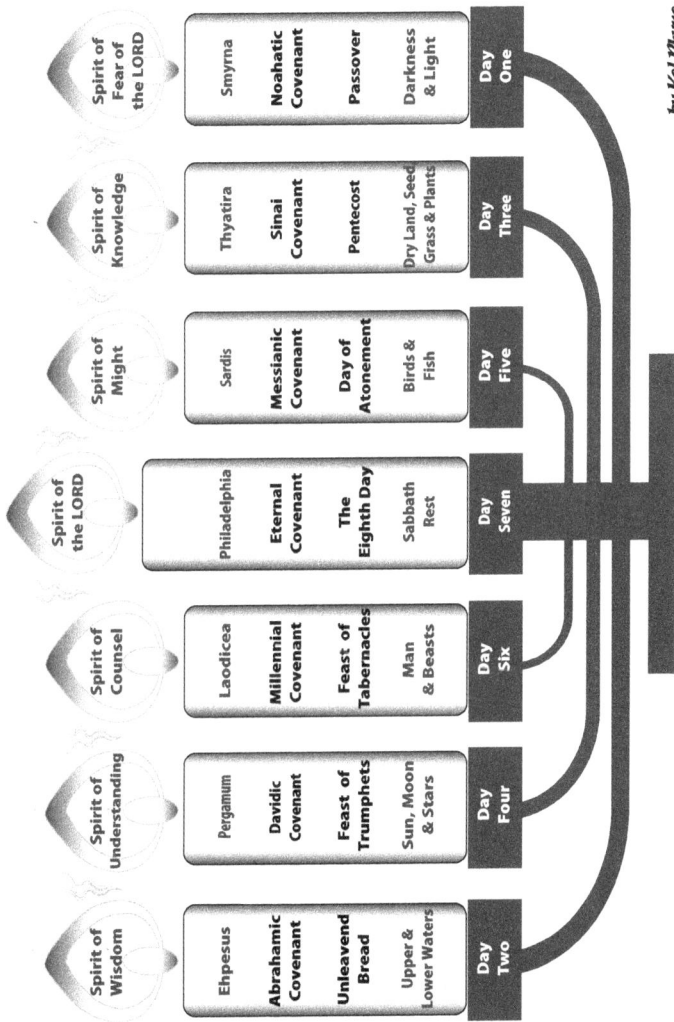

Spirit of Fear of the LORD	Spirit of Knowledge	Spirit of Might	Spirit of the LORD	Spirit of Counsel	Spirit of Understanding	Spirit of Wisdom
Smyrna	Thyatira	Sardis	Philadelphia	Laodicea	Pergamum	Ehpesus
Noahatic Covenant	Sinai Covenant	Messianic Covenant	Eternal Covenant	Millennial Covenant	Davidic Covenant	Abrahamic Covenant
Passover	Pentecost	Day of Atonement	The Eighth Day	Feast of Tabernacles	Feast of Trumpets	Unleavend Bread
Darkness & Light	Dry Land, Seed, Grass & Plants	Birds & Fish	Sabbath Rest	Man & Beasts	Sun, Moon & Stars	Upper & Lower Waters
Day One	Day Three	Day Five	Day Seven	Day Six	Day Four	Day Two

by Kel Rhyne

63

The 7 Fold Soul and 7 Body Systems of Man NOT Utilizing Positive Energies

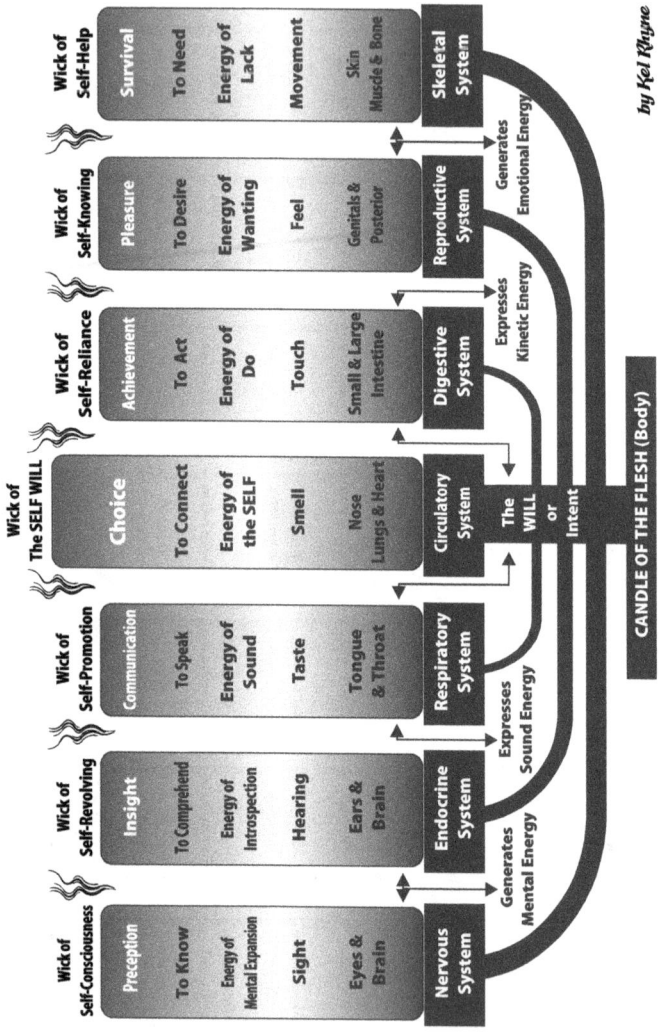

Wick of Self-Consciousness	Wick of Self-Revolving	Wick of Self-Promotion	Wick of The SELF WILL	Wick of Self-Reliance	Wick of Self-Knowing	Wick of Self-Help
Preception	Insight	Communication	Choice	Achievement	Pleasure	Survival
To Know	To Comprehend	To Speak	To Connect	To Act	To Desire	To Need
Energy of Mental Expansion	Energy of Introspection	Energy of Sound	Energy of the SELF	Energy of Do	Energy of Wanting	Energy of Lack
Sight	Hearing	Taste	Smell	Touch	Feel	Movement
Eyes & Brain	Ears & Brain	Tongue & Throat	Nose Lungs & Heart	Small & Large Intestine	Genitals & Posterior	Skin Muscle & Bone
Nervous System	Endocrine System	Respiratory System	Circulatory System	Digestive System	Reproductive System	Skeletal System

Generates Mental Energy

Expresses Sound Energy

Expresses Kinetic Energy

Generates Emotional Energy

The WILL or Intent

CANDLE OF THE FLESH (Body)

by Kel Rhyne

64

The 7 Fold Soul and 7 Body Systems of Man Utilizing Holy Fruit / Energies

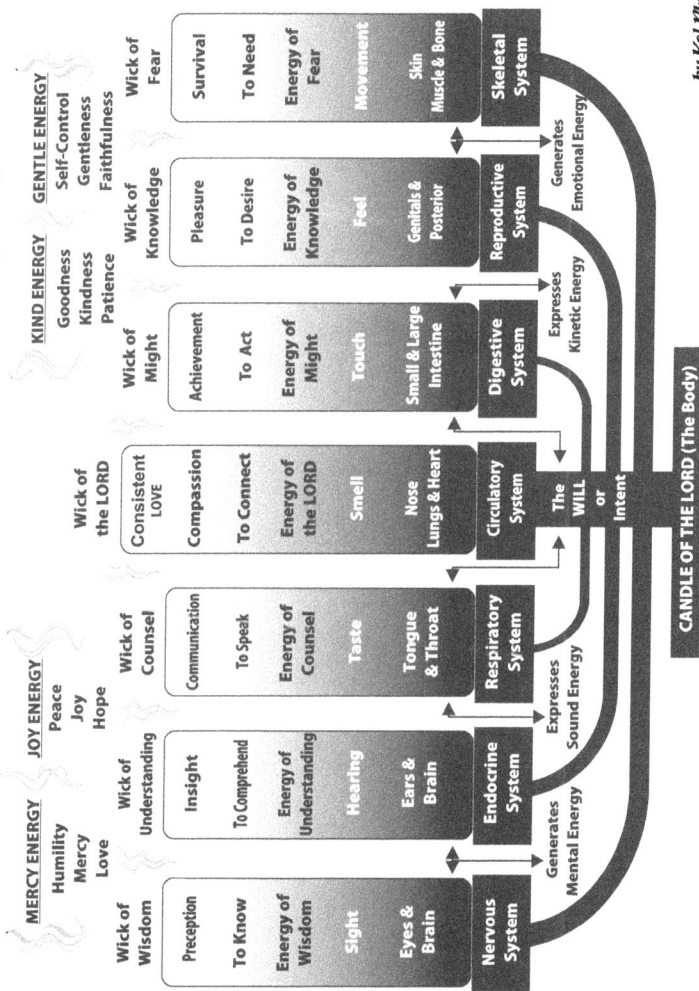

MERCY ENERGY	JOY ENERGY		KIND ENERGY	GENTLE ENERGY
Humility, Mercy, Love	Peace, Joy, Hope		Goodness, Kindness, Patience	Self-Control, Gentleness, Faithfulness

Wick of Wisdom	Wick of Understanding	Wick of Counsel	Wick of the LORD	Wick of Might	Wick of Knowledge	Wick of Fear
Preception	Insight	Communication	Consistent LOVE	Achievement	Pleasure	Survival
To Know	To Comprehend	To Speak	Compassion	To Act	To Desire	To Need
Energy of Wisdom	Energy of Understanding	Energy of Counsel	To Connect	Energy of Might	Energy of Knowledge	Energy of Fear
Sight	Hearing	Taste	Energy of the LORD	Touch	Feel	Movement
Eyes & Brain	Ears & Brain	Tongue & Throat	Smell	Small & Large Intestine	Genitals & Posterior	Skin Muscle & Bone
Nervous System	Endocrine System	Respiratory System	Nose Lungs & Heart	Digestive System	Reproductive System	Skeletal System
Generates Mental Energy	Expresses Sound Energy		Circulatory System	Expresses Kinetic Energy	Generates Emotional Energy	

The WILL or Intent

CANDLE OF THE LORD (The Body)

by Kel Rhyne

65

7 Fold Holy Spirit ~ 7 Fold Soul ~ 7 Body Systems

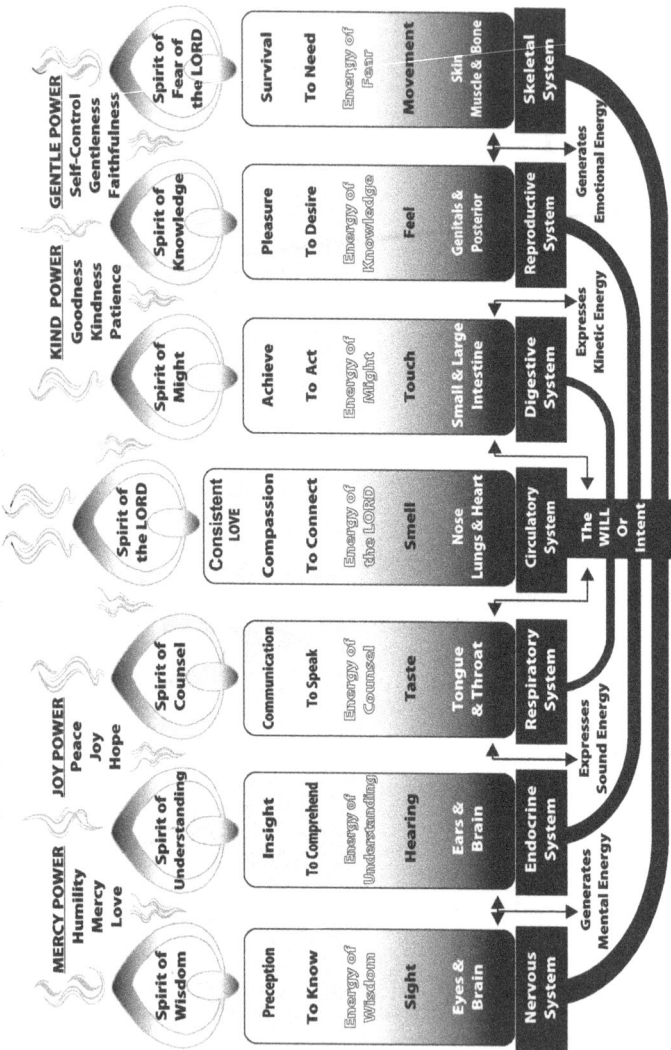

MERCY POWER Humility Mercy Love		JOY POWER Peace Joy Hope		KIND POWER Goodness Kindness Patience		GENTLE POWER Self-Control Gentleness Faithfulness
Spirit of Wisdom	Spirit of Understanding	Spirit of Counsel	Spirit of the LORD	Spirit of Might	Spirit of Knowledge	Spirit of Fear of the LORD
Preception	Insight	Communication	Consistent LOVE Compassion	Achieve	Pleasure	Survival
To Know	To Comprehend	To Speak	To Connect	To Act	To Desire	To Need
Energy of Wisdom	Energy of Understanding	Energy of Counsel	Energy of the LORD	Energy of Might	Energy of Knowledge	Energy of Fear
Sight	Hearing	Taste	Smell	Touch	Feel	Movement
Eyes & Brain	Ears & Brain	Tongue & Throat	Nose Lungs & Heart	Small & Large Intestine	Genitals & Posterior	Skin Muscle & Bone
Nervous System	Endocrine System	Respiratory System	Circulatory System	Digestive System	Reproductive System	Skeletal System
Generates Mental Energy		Expresses Sound Energy		Expresses Kinetic Energy	Generates Emotional Energy	

The WILL Or Intent

TEMPLE OF THE LORD (The Body)

by Kel Rhyne

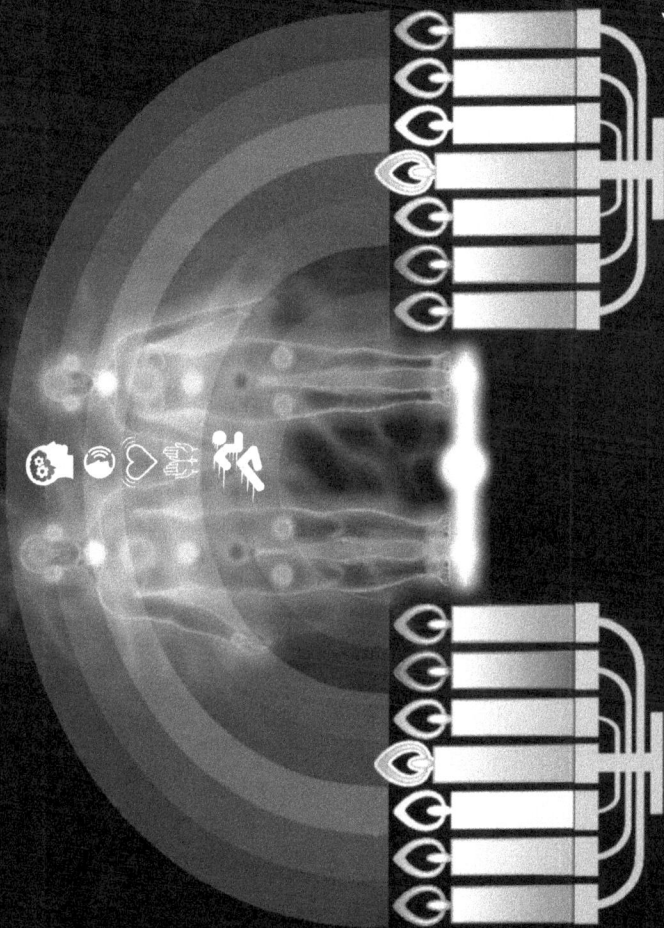

7 Soul Energies - Locations In The Body

by Kel Rhyne

The 7 Fold Soul
7 Energies of Man Operating as 5 Energies

Showing The Energy Flow
From Spirit > to Soul > to Expression

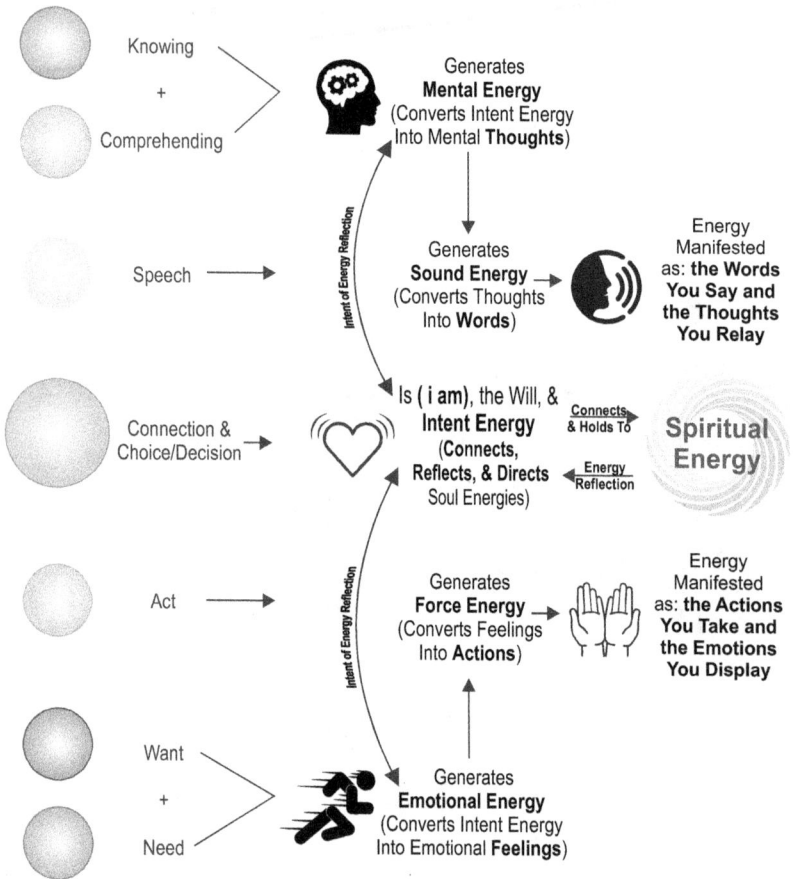

Knowing
+
Comprehending

Generates
Mental Energy
(Converts Intent Energy
Into Mental **Thoughts**)

Speech

Intent of Energy Reflection

Generates
Sound Energy
(Converts Thoughts
Into **Words**)

Energy
Manifested
as: **the Words
You Say and
the Thoughts
You Relay**

Connection &
Choice/Decision

Is (**i am**), the Will, &
Intent Energy
(**Connects,
Reflects, & Directs**
Soul Energies)

Connects
& Holds To

Energy
Reflection

**Spiritual
Energy**

Act

Intent of Energy Reflection

Generates
Force Energy
(Converts Feelings
Into **Actions**)

Energy
Manifested
as: **the Actions
You Take and
the Emotions
You Display**

Want
+
Need

Generates
Emotional Energy
(Converts Intent Energy
Into Emotional **Feelings**)

by Kel Rhyne

68

-The Spirit Mirror Chart- Man - The Image & Likeness of The Holy Invisible Yah

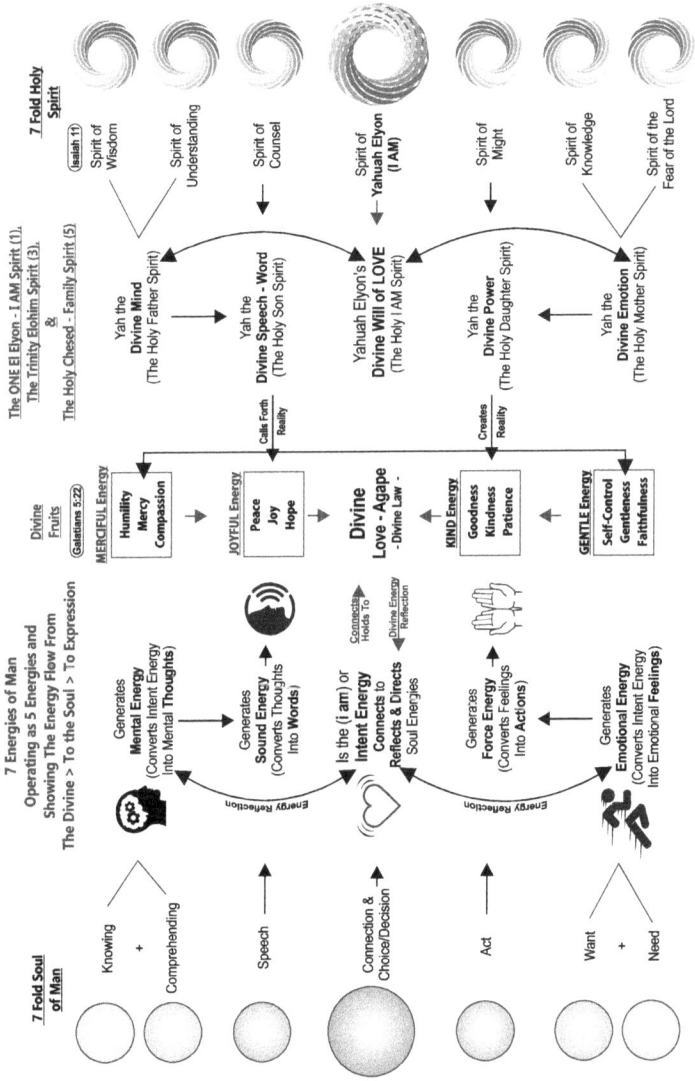

The ONE El Elyon - I AM Spirit (1),
The Trinity Elohim Spirit (3),
&
The Holy Chesed - Family Spirit (5)

7 Fold Holy Spirit
(Isaiah 11)

- Spirit of Wisdom
- Spirit of Understanding
- Spirit of Counsel
- Spirit of Yahuah Elyon (I AM)
- Spirit of Might
- Spirit of Knowledge
- Spirit of the Fear of the Lord

Yah the **Divine Mind** (The Holy Father Spirit)

Yah the **Divine Speech - Word** (The Holy Son Spirit)

Yahuah Elyon's **Divine Will of LOVE** (The Holy I AM Spirit)

Yah the **Divine Power** (The Holy Daughter Spirit)

Yah the **Divine Emotion** (The Holy Mother Spirit)

Calls Forth Reality

Creates Reality

Divine Fruits
(Galatians 5:22)

MERCIFUL Energy
- Humility
- Mercy
- Compassion

JOYFUL Energy
- Peace
- Joy
- Hope

Divine Love - Agape - Divine Law -

KIND Energy
- Goodness
- Kindness
- Patience

GENTLE Energy
- Self-Control
- Gentleness
- Faithfulness

7 Energies of Man
Operating as 5 Energies and
Showing The Energy Flow From
The Divine > To the Soul > To Expression

Generates **Mental Energy** (Converts Intent Energy Into Mental Thoughts)

Generates **Sound Energy** (Converts Thoughts Into Words)

Is the (I am) or **Intent Energy** Connects to Reflects & Directs Soul Energies

Connects Holds To / Divine Energy Reflection

Generates **Force Energy** (Converts Feelings Into Actions)

Generates **Emotional Energy** (Converts Intent Energy Into Emotional Feelings)

Energy Reflection

7 Fold Soul of Man

- Knowing + Comprehending
- Speech
- Connection & Choice/Decision
- Act
- Want + Need

69

12 Fruits of the Holy Spirit
Combined With The Soul Energies
To Develop "LOVE"

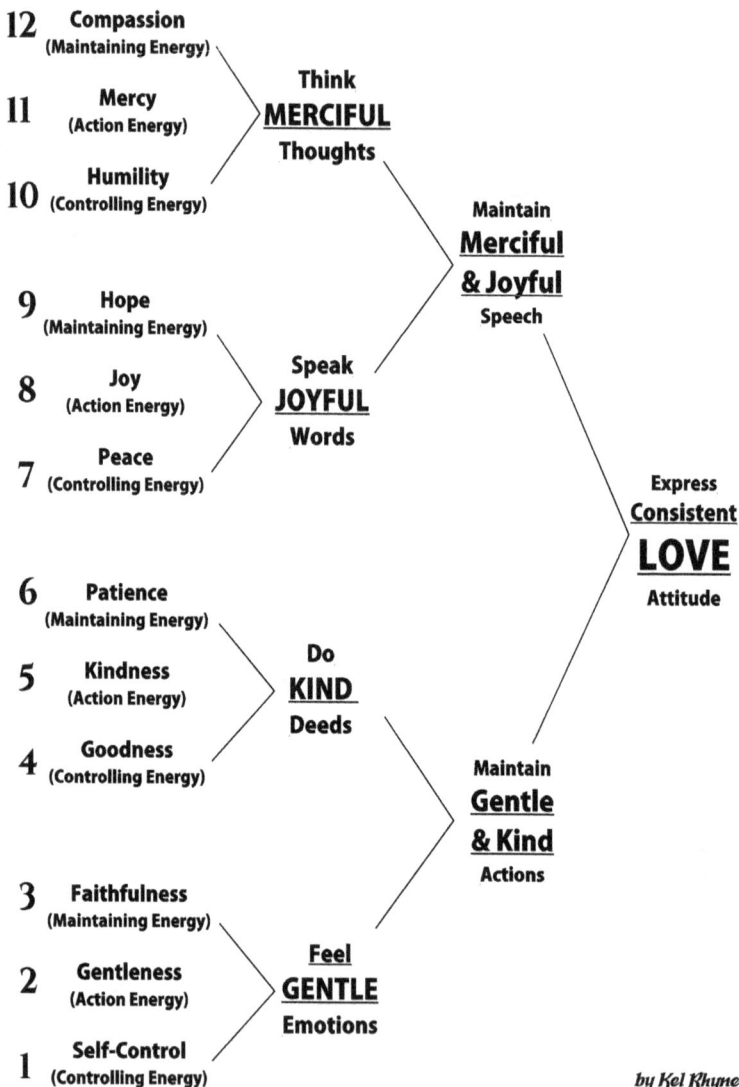

12 **Compassion**
(Maintaining Energy)

11 **Mercy**
(Action Energy)

10 **Humility**
(Controlling Energy)

Think
MERCIFUL
Thoughts

Maintain
Merciful
& Joyful
Speech

9 **Hope**
(Maintaining Energy)

8 **Joy**
(Action Energy)

7 **Peace**
(Controlling Energy)

Speak
JOYFUL
Words

Express
Consistent
LOVE
Attitude

6 **Patience**
(Maintaining Energy)

5 **Kindness**
(Action Energy)

4 **Goodness**
(Controlling Energy)

Do
KIND
Deeds

Maintain
Gentle
& Kind
Actions

3 **Faithfulness**
(Maintaining Energy)

2 **Gentleness**
(Action Energy)

1 **Self-Control**
(Controlling Energy)

Feel
GENTLE
Emotions

by Kel Rhyne

12 Holy Energies Summary

Consistent Love:

Consistent Love developed in a person is the shadow of Holy Love from Yah. It composes the center of Righteousness and is the very **WILL of Yahuah**. It is a deep, abiding love that is unwavering and long-lasting. It is not a fleeting emotion, but one that is rooted in commitment, loyalty, and trust. Yea, it is the sum total of all 12 Energies Combined! It is tenderness and understanding, acceptance and appreciation, kindness and patience. It is a love that is both practical and romantic, one that can weather difficult times and make even the darkest days seem brighter.

Consistent Love is also a powerful emotion, one that brings strength and joy to any relationship. It is a love that stands the test of time, one that is a source of comfort, security, and contentment. It is a love that is worth fighting for and cherishing, one that can make all the difference in the world, for it is the energy that holds together the very fabric of reality.

Compassion: the sympathetic consciousness of others' distress together with a desire to alleviate it.

Compassion is the ability to feel deep empathy for another person or creature and is often shown through actions such as offering help and support. This type of love is often considered to be one of the most important virtues and can be used to motivate others to do good.

Mercy: the compassion or forbearance shown especially to an offender or to one subject to one's power.

Mercy is the ability to show compassion and forgiveness towards others, even in the face of their worst actions. This showing of love is seen through actions such as lessening or absolving the punishment of offenders and extending to them forgiveness.

Humility: the freedom from pride or arrogance; the quality or state of being humble.

Humility is the ability to recognize and accept one's own limitations, and is often shown through actions such as being respectful towards others. This kind of love is a key component of maturity and is often seen as a key factor in building lasting relationships.

Hope: the holding of a desire or idea with anticipation and pleasant expectation.

Hope is the belief that despite the difficulties and obstacles in life, there is still a chance for happiness and success. This holding of love is shown through actions such as maintaining a positive outlook, and refusing to give up on dreams and goals.

Joy: the emotion evoked by well-being, success, or good fortune or by the prospect of possessing what one desires.

Joy is a feeling of happiness and satisfaction and is often shown through actions such as laughing and smiling. This expression of love is one of the most important emotions, and is often seen as a key factor in maintaining a positive attitude.

Peace: the active state of tranquility, stillness, and quietness.

Peace is a state of tranquility, and serenity, and is often shown through actions such as being patient and accepting of others. This presence of love is vital for happiness and well-being and can be used to prevent conflicts from arising.

Patience: the capacity of bearing pains and trials calmly and without complaint.

Patience is the ability to tolerate difficult conditions and situations and is often shown through actions such as waiting for an opportunity to arise. This waiting of love is a key factor in success and can be used to delay gratification in order to achieve goals.

Kindness: the quality or state of a sympathetic and helpful nature.

Kindness is the ability to be gentle and compassionate towards others and is often shown through actions such as helping others and being charitable. This disposition of love is also one of the most important virtues and can be used to build relationships and friendships.

Goodness: the quality or state of being good.

Goodness is the moral quality of doing good and being kind and is often shown through actions such as being respectful and polite. This form of love is a foundational component of morality and can be used to motivate others to do good.

Faithfulness: the quality of being steadfast in affection or allegiance.

Faithfulness is the ability to keep promises and commitments, and is often shown through actions such as being faithful to one's friends and loved ones. This continuation of love is an essential energy and is one of the most important virtues it is used to build trust and relationships.

Gentleness: the state of being calm, smooth, and easy going.

Gentleness is characterized by warmth, forgiveness, and empathy. This quality makes it a desirable trait in a person. It is also important for moral values because it shows that someone is able to regulate their own emotions and behavior. This attribute makes gentleness high in moral value.

Self-Control: the state of restraint exercised over one's own impulses, emotions, and desires.

Self-control is the ability to refrain from acting on impulses or desires, especially when those impulses or desires are considered morally wrong. It is important for our spiritual growth, it is a quality that is highly valued and is the foundation on which other virtues can grow. If we are able to control our impulses, we are more likely to learn and grow. This is especially important in the spiritual discipline of meditation and prayer.

Lastly, self-control is important for our relationships. If we are able to control our emotions, we are less likely to hurt or anger our friends and loved ones. This is especially important in relationships where emotions are frequently expressed physically.

Order Of Melchizedek

From Enoch to Methuselah to Lamech to Noah to Shem who
(received Noah's Mantle and the Book of Healings & Demonic Reversals) became Melchizedek

Melchizedek Priesthood - Mazdaism - Magi

Most High God - Ahru Mazda

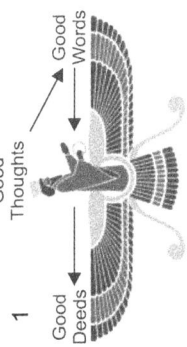

1

Good Thoughts
Good Words
Good Deeds

(Revised / More Full) Melchizedek Priesthood

Most High God - Yahuah Elohim

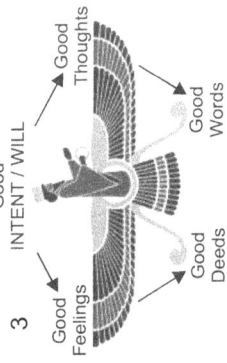

3

Good INTENT / WILL
Good Thoughts
Good Words
Good Deeds
Good Feelings

Melchizedek HIGH Priest - King Yahusha

Most High God - Yahuah Elyon - Yahuah Elohim

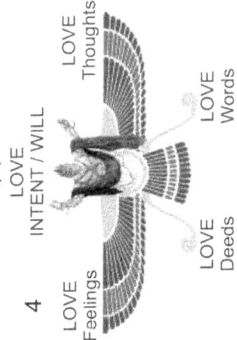

4

LOVE INTENT / WILL
LOVE Thoughts
LOVE Words
LOVE Deeds
LOVE Feelings

Abraham was blessed by Melchizedek, but did not receive his mantle as priest. The *Melchizedek Priesthood* is NOT from Israel, however, it can be traced to Persia (*Iran*). This Order of Priests know as *Magi*, are those who read the constellations and followed the North Star to find baby Yahusha. Their religion today is called Mazdaism (*Zoroastrianism*).

The Soul Of Man

Yahuah - Yahusha - Will Of LOVE

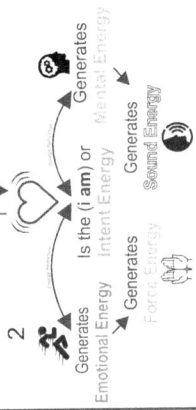

2

Generates Emotional Energy
Generates Force Energy
Is the (i am) or Intent Energy
Generates Mental Energy
Generates Sound Energy

The Soul Of Man

Vertical Layout and Energy Flow

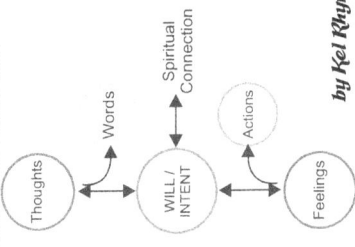

Thoughts
Words
WILL / INTENT
Spiritual Connection
Actions
Feelings

by Kel Rhyne

75

The Kingdom Of Yah's Governing Priesthood

Matthew 5:17-19
Think not that I am come to destroy the law, or the prophets: I am not come to destroy, but to *Fulfill*...
Whosoever therefore shall break one of these least commandments, and shall teach men so, he shall be called the **Least** in the kingdom of heaven: but whosoever shall do and teach them, the same shall be called **Great** in the kingdom of heaven.

Peter 2:9
"you are a chosen people, a **Royal Priesthood**..."

Revelation 1:6
"and has made us **Kings and Priests** unto Elohim."

Hebrew 5:6 - Psalm 110:4
Yahuah has sworn and will not change his mind: "You are a priest forever, in *the order of Melchizedek.*"

---

3 Classes of Priests
Lesser Priests - Greater Priests - Royal Priests

1. **Lesser Priest** - foreshadowed as: *the Order of Levi*

Under the Covenant of Yahusha... this class of priests are composed of those who engage in the Covenant of Yahusha for the forgiveness of sins. They strive to *live and teach* His "Gospel" as best as they understand... rightly so, Yahusha is faithful and just to forgive them of their sins... they will take part in the 1st Resurrection by being raised from the dead at Yahusha's return to inherit the Kingdom as "*Least*" (of the Governing Saints) in the Kingdom.

2. **Greater Priest** - foreshadowed as: *the Order of Aaron*

Under the Covenant of Yahusha ... this class of priests are composed of those who engage in the Covenant of Yahusha for the forgiveness of sin, however, they go back into the "Law" striving to *live and teach* the commands & precepts therein... this is commendable! For Yahusha's Covenant has its roots in the Torah. They will take part in the 1st Resurrection by being raised from the dead at Yahusha's return to inherit the Kingdom as "*Great*" (of the Governing Saints) in the Kingdom.

3. **Royal Priest** - foreshadowed as: *the Order of Melchizedek*

Under the Covenant of Yahusha... this class of priest, like the first group, engages the Covenant of Yahusha for the forgiveness of sins... like the second group, they understand that their current Covenant has its roots in "Torah"... however, they focus less on trying to keep the previous covenant laws, and move forward placing their intent on striving to *live and teach* Yahusha's Covenant; for it is Yahusha's Covenant that they were Baptized into. This Covenant is fulfilled through the guidance and fullness of the Holy Spirit! They will take part in the 1st Resurrection. Those who have *been slain* will be resurrected and those who are divinely protected during the Great Tribulation will be raised to meet Yahusha in the air at His return. This group will have their *Mortality* changed to *Immortality* in the twinkling of an eye and will inherit the Kingdom as "*Royal*" (of the Governing Saints) in the Kingdom. 144,000+.

1 Corinthians 15:51-54
Behold, I tell you a mystery: We shall not all sleep, but we shall all be changed— in a moment, in the twinkling of an eye, at the last trumpet. For the trumpet will sound, and the dead will be raised incorruptible, and we shall be changed. For this corruptible must put on incorruption, and this mortal must put on immortality. So when this corruptible has put on incorruption, and this mortal has put on immortality, then shall be brought to pass the saying that is written: "Death is swallowed up in victory."

MAY:

"**Yahuah** bless you and guard you;
Yahuah make His face shine upon you,
And be gracious to you;
Yahuah lift up His countenance upon you,
And give you peace." _Numbers 6:24-26_

Go ye therefore and teach all nations,
baptizing them in the name of

"Yahuah"

and of

"Yahusha"

and of

"Yah Qodesh"

Matthew 28:19

Journey On!

2 the Kingdom!